ABCEDAR

An Alphabet of Trees

by George Ella Lyon
designed and illustrated by Tom Parker

858114

Orchard Books / New York
a division of Franklin Watts, Inc.

A B C D E F G H I J K L M

Orchard Books, 387 Park Avenue South, New York, New York 10016
Orchard Books Great Britain, 10 Golden Square, London W1R 3AF England
Orchard Books Australia, 14 Mars Road, Lane Cove, New South Wales, 2066
Orchard Books Canada, 20 Torbay Road, Markham, Ontario 23P 1G6

Orchard Books is a division of Franklin Watts, Inc.

Manufactured in the United States of America.
The text of this book is set in Futura Extra Bold.
The illustrations are India ink with photo-mechanically applied colors.

10 9 8 7 6 5 4 3 2 1

Library of Congress Cataloging-in-Publication Data
Lyon, George Ella, 1949-
A B Cedar: an alphabet of trees / by George Ella Lyon;
designed and illustrated by Tom Parker.
Summary: An alphabet book introducing the leaves from a variety of trees.
ISBN 0-531-05795-X.   ISBN 0-531-08395-0 (lib. bdg.)
1. Trees—Identification—Juvenile literature. 2. Leaves—Identification—
Juvenile literature. 3. English language—Alphabet—Juvenile literature. [1.
Trees—Identification. 2. Leaves—Identification. 3. Alphabet.]
I. Parker, Tom, ill. II. Title.

QK477.2.I4L96 1989   582.16—dc19   [E]
88-22797 CIP AC

NOPQRSTUVWXYZ

In memory of my grandfather, J.D. Fowler, who knew trees,
and Jamie Duke, who loved letters.

G.E.L.

A B C D E F G H I J K L M

NOPQRSTUVWXYZ

A B C D E F G H I J K L

ABCDEFGHIJ M

PQRSTUV KYZ

TEAK

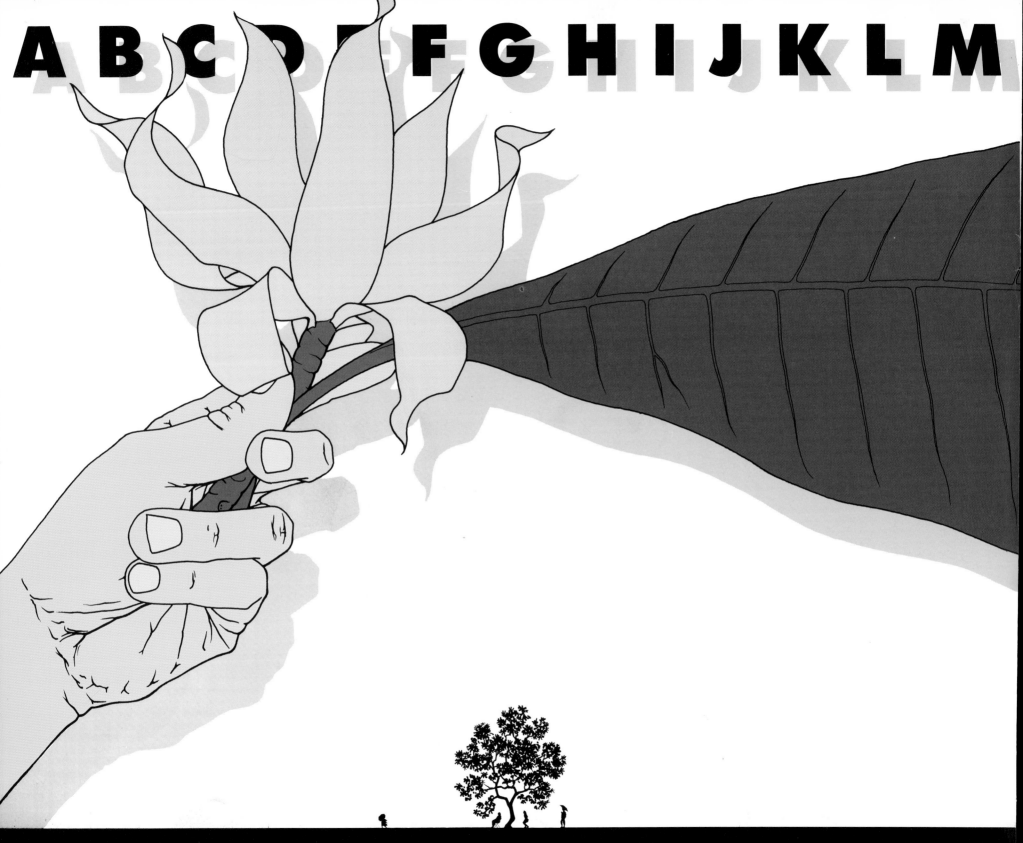

A B C D E F G H I J K L M

UMBRELLA TREE

Air and food   Shade and wood

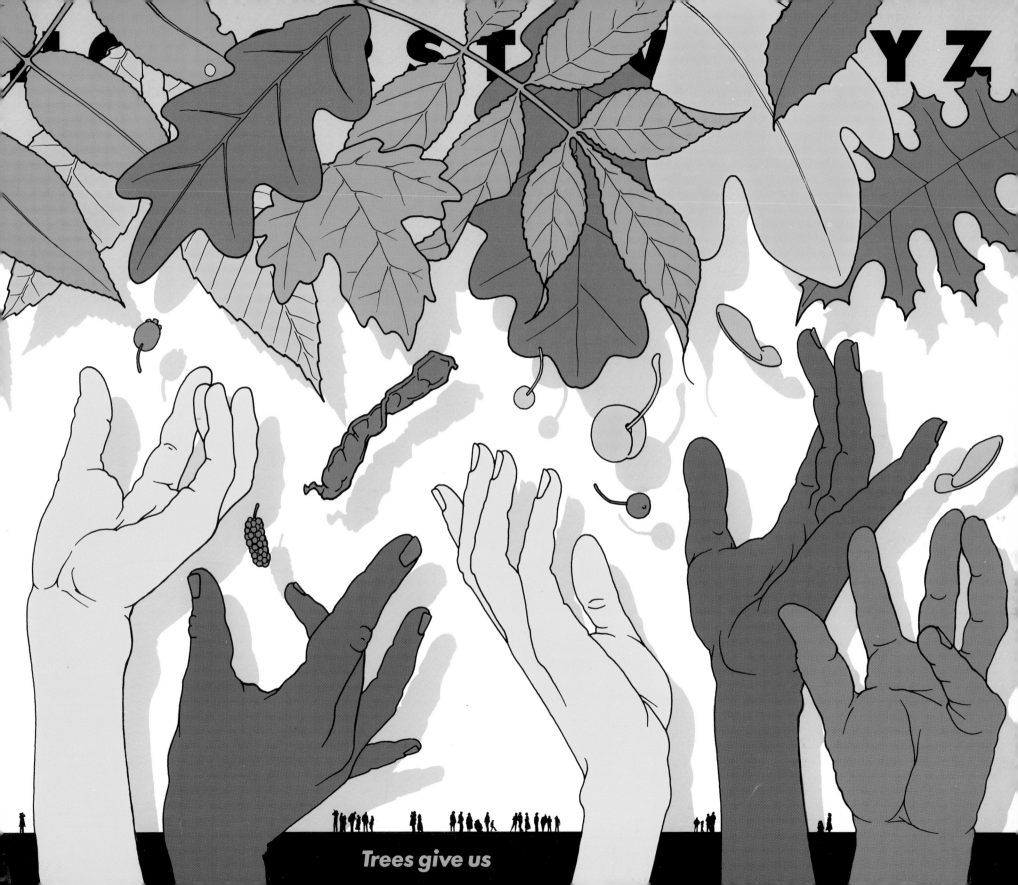

Trees give us